HISTORY
OF THE WORLD

FIRST CITIES AND EMPIRES

10,000BCE to 476CE

by John Farndon
Illustrated by Christian Cornia

HUNGRY
TOMATO™

HISTORY OF THE WORLD
FIRST CITIES AND EMPIRES
10,000BCE to 476CE

Thanks to the creative team:

Senior Editor: Alice Peebles
Consultant: John Haywood
Fact checking: Tom Jackson
Design: www.collaborate agency

First published in Great Britain in 2018
by Hungry Tomato Ltd
PO Box 181
Edenbridge
Kent, TN8 9DP

A CIP catalogue record for this book is
available from the British Library.

ISBN 978-1-912108-69-5

Printed and bound in China

Discover more at
www.hungrytomato.com

CONTENTS

In the book, 'mya' is used for 'million years ago', and 'ya' for 'years ago'; c. before a date means *circa* or 'about', showing a precise date is not known.

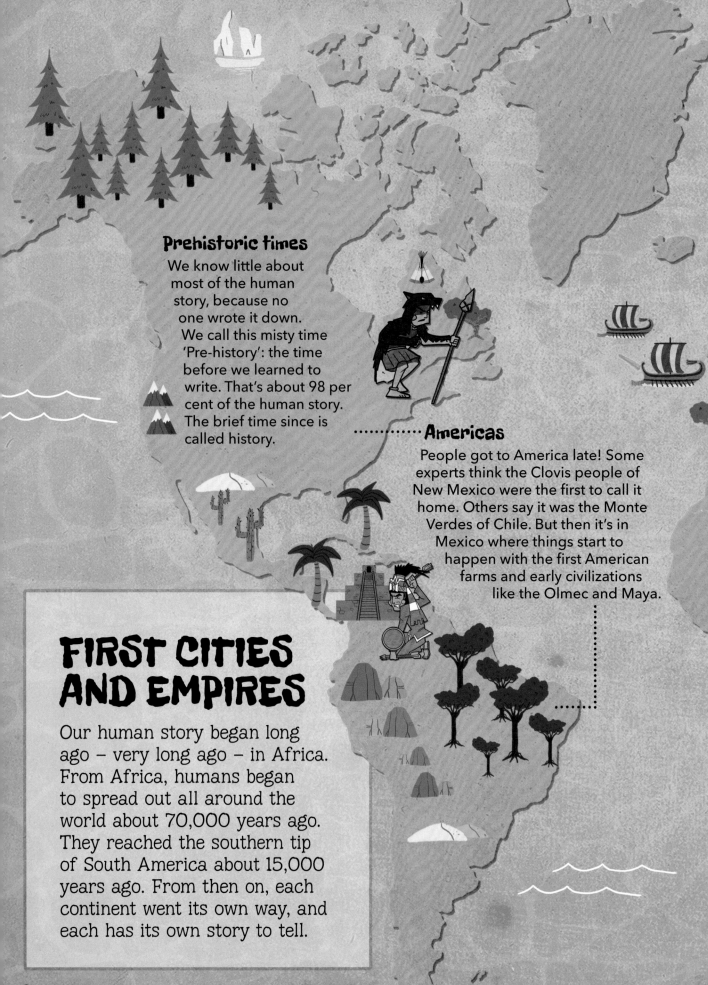

Prehistoric times

We know little about most of the human story, because no one wrote it down. We call this misty time 'Pre-history': the time before we learned to write. That's about 98 per cent of the human story. The brief time since is called history.

Americas

People got to America late! Some experts think the Clovis people of New Mexico were the first to call it home. Others say it was the Monte Verdes of Chile. But then it's in Mexico where things start to happen with the first American farms and early civilizations like the Olmec and Maya.

FIRST CITIES AND EMPIRES

Our human story began long ago – very long ago – in Africa. From Africa, humans began to spread out all around the world about 70,000 years ago. They reached the southern tip of South America about 15,000 years ago. From then on, each continent went its own way, and each has its own story to tell.

Asia

What happened in Mesopotamia happened, too, in India and especially China: the discovery of metals and farming and the first great cities and writing. And while civilizations in Europe and Eurasia came and went, China's has endured for thousands of years.

Europe

For a long time, it was seriously cold in the north because of the Ice Age! People were mostly hunters, then simple farmers. But about 2,500 years ago, civilization kicked off in the south: first the amazing Greeks with their ideas, then the Romans with their huge legions and mighty empire.

Eurasia

The 'Fertile Land' extends from Egypt into Iraq. Here, people probably first began farming. In the east, along the Tigris and Euphrates rivers, was Mesopotamia (modern Iraq). History began here, with the first writing and the first civilizations, such as the Sumerian.

Africa

Although we humans began in Africa, much of it stayed prehistoric. But in the north-east along the Nile, the astonishing Ancient Egyptian civilization appeared over 5,000 years ago. It lasted 3,000 years under its kings or 'pharaohs'. They built awe-inspiring pyramids and statues – and developed one of the first-ever writing systems.

Australia

The first Australians, the aboriginals, arrived in Australia some 55,000 years ago. The land could not be farmed until 250 years ago, when Europeans arrived with crops and domestic animals.

Dark arts
40-20,000 ya Eurasia

During the Stone Age, people painted on cave walls. There are many paintings of animals such as horses and bison. The most famous cave paintings are at Lascaux in France.

35,000–25,000 years ago

Pointing finger
600,000-40,000 ya Siberia

For a while, we humans shared the world with creatures a bit like us called Neanderthals and Denisovans. But we know of Denisovans from little more than an old finger found in a Siberian cave.

● **Denisova Cave, Altai Mountains**

40,000 years ago

● **Lascaux**

● **Beijing**

100,000–90,000 years ago

150,000–100,000 years ago

We're only human
From 200,000 ya Africa

The great grandma of us all lived in Africa 200,000 years ago. About 70,000 years ago, her offspring trekked out of Africa and spread around the world. The arrows on the map show where they went first.

● **Olduvai, Tanzania**

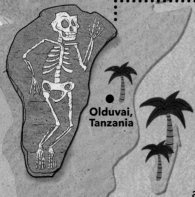

60,000–50,000 years ago

Uluru/Ayers Rock

The First Aussies *55,000 ya Australia*

Around 55,000 years ago, a few people bravely crossed the open sea from Indonesia on rafts to reach Australia. Their descendants are the aboriginal Australians of today.

2.6 MYA	2 MYA	1 MYA	0.6 MYA	0.5 MYA	200,000 YA
First stone tools made	*Homo erectus* migrates from Africa	First controlled use of fire	Neanderthal people arrive in Europe	First spears made	First humans

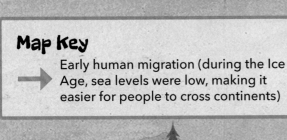

Map Key

→ Early human migration (during the Ice Age, sea levels were low, making it easier for people to cross continents)

16,000 years ago

The First Americans

13,000 ya North America

Humans arrived in North America from Siberia. Among them were the Clovis people. They are called Clovis people because their stone tools have been found at Clovis, New Mexico.

Clovis, New Mexico ●

THE AGE OF STONE
More than 12,000 years ago

Long ago, our ancestors lived in the wild, hunting animals and gathering fruit for food. They slept in caves or up trees, and often went on long treks to find food. Their only real tools were sharpened stones. That's why this is called the Stone Age – obviously.

14,000 years ago

170,000 YA	71,000 YA	70,000 YA	50,000 YA	42,000 YA	15,000 YA
First clothes from animal skins	First bows and arrows	Humans leave Africa	Sewing invented	The world's oldest flute	Monte Verde people settle in Chile

9

Melting ice
11,700 ya N Europe and America

For 1.8 mlllion years, there was an Ice Age and the far north of Europe and America was supercold! The land was covered in really thick ice. Then about 11,700 years ago, it finally got warmer and the ice melted...

Long in the Tooth
12,000 ya North America

Soon after humans arrived in North America, some large kinds of animal died out, such as sabre-toothed cats and mammoths. Maybe human hunters killed them all, but no one really knows.

Jomon the rangers
Over 12,000 ya Japan

The Jomons lived in Japan until about 3,000 years ago. They were hunters and gatherers, but because there was so much fruit, fish and game, they had time to build houses and make pots.

SETTLING DOWN
12,000-9,000 years ago

Maybe because wild food was scarce, some people got fed up with wandering about. They settled down to produce their food by farming instead. They even started to live in houses and towns.

12,000 YA Goats domesticated	**12,000 YA** Jomon pottery made in Japan	**11,700 YA** Ice Age ends	**c.11,500 YA** Farming of wheat and barley	**c.11,000 YA** New Stone Age begins	**11,000 YA** Sheep domesticated

China rice 12,000 ya China

Different crops were started in different places. In China, they grew rice over 12,000 years ago. By 6,300 years ago, the Chinese found it grew really well in flooded fields called paddies.

Logging out
10,000 ya Netherlands

People may have crossed the sea in boats 130,000 years ago. But the oldest boat ever found is a 10,000-year-old canoe scooped from a log, preserved in mud at Pesse in the Netherlands.

Pesse

Çatalhöyük

ANATOLIA

Jericho

MESOPOTAMIA

JORDAN

The oldest town?
9,500 ya Turkey

Soon people built houses together in towns such as Çatalhöyük in Turkey. Çatalhöyük didn't have any streets. You just walked over your neighbour's flat roof and climbed down into your house!

The first farmers
11,500 ya Syria

People eventually realized you didn't have to search for wild plants – you could just plant seeds and grow them on the spot as crops. Their first successes were wheat, barley, lentils and types of peas.

Arty farmers
10,300 ya Jordan

Hunters and gatherers had to travel light. But once people settled in villages to farm, they could make lots of things to decorate their homes, like these odd statues from Ain Ghazal in Jordan.

11,000 YA	10,800 YA	10,000 YA	9,500 YA	9,000 YA	9,000 YA
The oldest temple: Göbekli Tepe, Turkey	City of Byblos built in the Lebanon	Many animals become extinct	Fertile parts of the Sahara are farmed	Tower built in Jericho	Jiahu culture begins in China

11

Stonehenge, Britain 5,000 ya

Carnac standing stones, France 6,500 ya

Louisiana mounds
5,400–2,700 ya Louisiana

Long before cities, Stone Age people built monuments from mounds and rings of earth, like those at Watson Brake in Louisiana, and later, Poverty Point (shown). Why they did this is a mystery…

THE FIRST CITIES
9,000–6,000 years ago

Once farming began, life got a whole lot more complicated! People started owning land and selling crops to buy tools and things. And soon the first cities grew as places for markets and for governments to organize it all. This is called civilization.

Ring time
7,000 ya Egypt

At Nabta Playa, people set up a circle of stones that align with the sun and stars at certain times of year. Similar ancient stone 'calendar' circles, such as Britain's Stonehenge, are found across Europe.

8,500 YA Copper mined in Timna, Israel	**8,000 YA** Aleppo in Syria first settled	**8,000 YA** Symbols made on tortoiseshell, China	**8,000 YA** Copper ornaments made in Pakistan	**7,500 YA** Copper smelted for tools in Serbia	**7,500 YA** Copper Age begins in Europe and Middle East

Going horse
6,000–5,000 ya Kazakhstan

For all of the Stone Age, people had to go everywhere slowly on foot. Then somewhere in central Asia about 5,500 years ago, someone had the bright idea of riding a horse. On a horse, people could get places, fast…

Copper Age
7,500 ya Serbia

From about 7,500 ya, stone was history. People discovered metals! With heat, you can make metals any shape you want. It all started with copper, like this axe found in Pločnik in Serbia.

Mehrgarh

Civilized
6,000 ya Iraq

The first cities were the centres of the first great civilizations. Ur, with its famous temple mound or 'ziggurat', was one of the chief cities of the Sumerian civilization in what is now southern Iraq.

Indian beginnings
8,500 ya India

The first proper villages in India appeared at Mehrgarh in Balochistan. There the people made strange statues, the oldest in southern Asia.

7,300 YA	**7,200 YA**	**7,000 YA**	**6,600 YA**	**6,500 YA**	**6,070 YA**
Tablets in Romania, the first writing?	Cave settlements on Malta	Eridu in Sumeria, perhaps the first city	Gold ornaments made in Bulgaria	Carnac stones erected in France	Trypillian people live in towns in Ukraine

Scary brave

3200BCE Western Europe

At Skara Brae in the Scottish Orkney islands, people built cosy stone houses. These were buried by sand until uncovered by a storm in 1850.

Rock around

2000BCE Western Europe

Stone Age Britons stood big stones or 'megaliths' upright, making the ring called Stonehenge in Wiltshire, England. Gaps in the stones seem to line up with the sun at times, but no one knows why...

Mound for the dead

3300BCE North America

Early farmers made special burial mounds for their dead. The 'Laurel people' of Manitoba, Canada, did this at Kay-Nah-Chi-Wah-Nung ('place of the long rapids').

EGYPT ARRIVES

4000-2600BCE

By 6,000 years ago, many people were settling down to farm and live in villages with houses made from wood, mud and stone. Some built amazing monuments to the dead and to gods. Great cities and civilizations appeared in the Middle East, China and Egypt.

4000BCE	3800BCE	3700BCE	3500BCE	3300BCE	3200BCE
Domestication of chickens	Wooden causeway laid in England	Minoan culture begins in Crete desert	First Egyptian mummies made	Newgrange burial mound in Ireland	Writing invented in Sumer

Far gone Sargon
c.2330BCE Middle East

King Sargon the Great (with the help of a few soldiers!) created one of the first great empires: the Akkadian Empire, by the Tigris and Euphrates rivers (modern Iraq).

AKKADIAN EMPIRE

Legendary leader
2697BCE China

Huangdi, the Yellow Emperor, is supposed to have kick-started Chinese civilization (if he existed!). His reign is said to have brought wooden houses, carts, boats, the bow and arrow, and writing. Legend says his wife discovered how to make silk.

Egypt is go!
3100BCE Africa

Ancient Egypt civilization began when farmers by the Nile were united by King Narmer the Catfish (really!). Some 170 kings or 'pharaohs' followed Narmer and ruled a civilization lasting 3,000 years.

3200BCE	**3200**BCE	**3000**BCE	**3000**BCE	**3000**BCE	**2600**BCE
Norte Chico culture flourishes in Peru	Skara Brae houses built in Scotland	Longshan culture begins in China	Stonehenge built in England	Papyrus (paper) made from reeds	Gilgamesh is king in Sumer

Big bang
1646BCE

The gigantic eruption of the Santorini volcano in Greece about 3,600 years ago blew the existing island out of the water. It then sent out a tidal wave said to have utterly destroyed the ancient Minoan civilization there.

THE AGE OF BRONZE
2600-1600BCE

Copper is too soft to make good tools and weapons. But about 4,600 years ago, someone found that if you add a little tin and arsenic to copper it you create super tough bronze – and the world moved into the Bronze Age.

Maya people

The Maya
2000BCE-1697CE Belize

About 4,000 years ago, the Maya began building the first great American civilization. They started as farmers growing maize and beans. But they also made amazing statues like this.

c.2600BCE	c.2300BCE	2200BCE	2200-2101BCE	2000BCE	2000BCE
Harappa a major city in Indus Valley	Sargon founds Akkadian Empire	Stonehenge in Britain completed	Mythical Yu emperor in China	Maya culture starts in Yucatán, Mexico	Bantu people migrate south from west Africa

No stink
3300-1300 BCE Pakistan

The people of the ancient cities of the Indus valley knew how to keep clean! They had the first-ever flush toilets and proper drains for washing away poo. Other old cities just stank!

First ruler?
2200-2101 BCE China

Yu the Great was the first ruler of China, legend says. Legend also says he solved China's problems with floods by digging canals to divert the water on to fields to help crops grow.

AKKADIAN EMPIRE

Babylon

ANCIENT EGYPT

● Memphis

INDUS VALLEY CIVILIZATION

Mighty mound
c.2550 BCE AFRICA

Egyptian civilization began some 5,100 years ago. Their powerful pharaohs (kings) built vast triangular stone tombs we call pyramids. The biggest ever was built for Pharaoh Khufu. It's over 140 m (460 ft) tall.

Ancient book
1700 BCE India

The Rig Veda was one of the first books, ever. It was a book of hymns, and the title means roughly 'Yeah – knowledge!' It's one of the key books for the Hindu religion.

2000 BCE	**1850** BCE	**1750** BCE	**1700** BCE	**1700** BCE	**1700** BCE
Kingdom of Kush begins in Africa	First alphabet from Sinai, Egypt	Erlitou Palace is built in China,	Rig Veda written	Poverty Point culture, USA	Babylon is the first megacity

THE AGE OF MYTHS

1600–750BCE

Later, as people began to settle down for a quiet life in cities, they loved to tell stories of this time when life was tougher and more exciting, and great heroes were made. It's hard to tell what is myth and what is true.

Hallstatt
1000BCE Europe

The Hallstatt people were Celts living in west and central Europe. They made fantastic spearheads, swords and axes from the new metal, iron.

Olympics
776BCE–393CE Greece

The Ancient Greeks loved sport and the very first Olympic Games are thought to have been held at Olympia in 776BCE. They were then held every four years for the next 1,200 years…

Big heads
1000BCE Mexico

The Olmec people created one of the first great civilizations in the Americas. But they are mostly famous for the 'colossal' stone heads they carved and left lying around in the jungles of Mexico.

Olmec La Venta

1600BCE	1600BCE	1600BCE	1600BCE	c.1500BCE	1279BCE
Shang dynasty starts in China	Mycenae dominate Greece	Hittite Empire begins	Chinese writing develops	Biblical prophet Moses	Ramesses the Great becomes Pharaoh

Wooden horse 1250BCE Turkey

The Greeks told stories about their wars to rescue beautiful Helen from the city of Troy, and of heroes such as Achilles. The best told of fooling the people of Troy into taking in a huge wooden horse containing soldiers, who then opened the city gates to the Greeks.

Dragon bones
1200BCE China

Fortune tellers in China wrote questions on slivers of bone and burnt them to see how they cracked. Millions of these bones survive, and they're the first bits of Chinese writing. They're called 'dragon bones' but are really oxbones.

Halstatt people

Carthage

Thebes

Hattusa

HITTITE EMPIRE

Nineveh

ASSYRIAN EMPIRE

Akhetaten, capital city of Akhenaten

Queen of the Nile

1350BCE Egypt

With her husband Akhenaten, the beautiful Egyptian queen, Nefertiti, started a revolution in Egypt. They led the idea that people should worship just one god, Amun, rather than many.

Big hitters

400CE Turkey, Iraq

From 1,600 to 1,180 years ago, the two big players in what is now Turkey and Iraq were the Hittites and Assyrians. Both built large empires with armies who fought with iron swords, spears and chariots.

| **1200BCE** Iron Age begins in Anatolia | **1046BCE** In China, Wu the Zhou overthrows the Shang | **900BCE** Chavin people flourish in Peru | **850BCE** Scythian horse warriors in Kazakhstan | **800BCE** Iron Age begins in Britain | **800BCE** Greek city-states develop |

Romulus and Remus
753BCE Italy

Legend says Romulus, the first king of Rome, was reared by wolves in a forest with his twin Remus. But by 500BCE, Rome no longer had a king and became a Republic.

The Lawgiver
reigned 590-560BCE Persia (Iran)

Cyrus the Great was the warrior hero whose victories created the Persian Empire. But he was also a ruler whose wise words, carved on a column outside Babylon, sit in the United Nations building even today.

Rome

Carthage

FIRST PERSIAN EMPIRE

Babylon

Thinking Greeks
500-323BCE

'Classical' Greece was on fire with ideas from poets such as Homer, and philosophers such as Plato and Aristotle. The Greeks revolutionized art with their beautiful lifelike statues and perfectly proportioned temples such as the Parthenon in Athens (above).

Zapotec 700BCE Mexico

It wasn't just in Egypt that people built pyramids and learnt to write in symbols and pictures. The Zapotec people of Oaxaca in Mexico did that too, entirely self-taught…

Monte Albán, Oaxaca

776BCE	745BCE	660BCE	563BCE	551BCE	539BCE
First Olympic Games	Start of the Assyrian Empire	In Japan, Jimmu is the first emperor	Prince Siddartha (Buddha) born	Confucius born in China	Cyrus the Great conquers Babylon

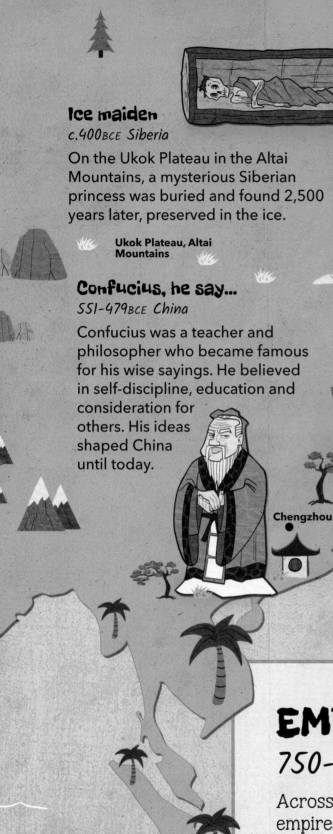

Ice maiden
c.400 BCE Siberia

On the Ukok Plateau in the Altai Mountains, a mysterious Siberian princess was buried and found 2,500 years later, preserved in the ice.

Ukok Plateau, Altai Mountains

Confucius, he say...
551-479 BCE China

Confucius was a teacher and philosopher who became famous for his wise sayings. He believed in self-discipline, education and consideration for others. His ideas shaped China until today.

Chengzhou

Jimmu
711-586 BCE Japan

Jimmu was the legendary first emperor of Japan. Legend says he was a great hero who led his small band of warrior outlaws to victory, using his skill with a bow.

EMPIRES AND IDEAS
750-400 BCE

Across the world, powerful rulers built empires like the Persian Empire. But in Greece, scholars, writers and artists changed the world for ever with their ideas alone.

522 BCE	**509 BCE**	**508 BCE**	**490 BCE**	**480 BCE**	**400 BCE**
Darius the Great is king of Persia	Roman Republic founded	Democracy starts in Athens, Greece	Major defeat of the Persians by Greeks	Persians conquer Greece	Zapotec culture thrives in Mexico

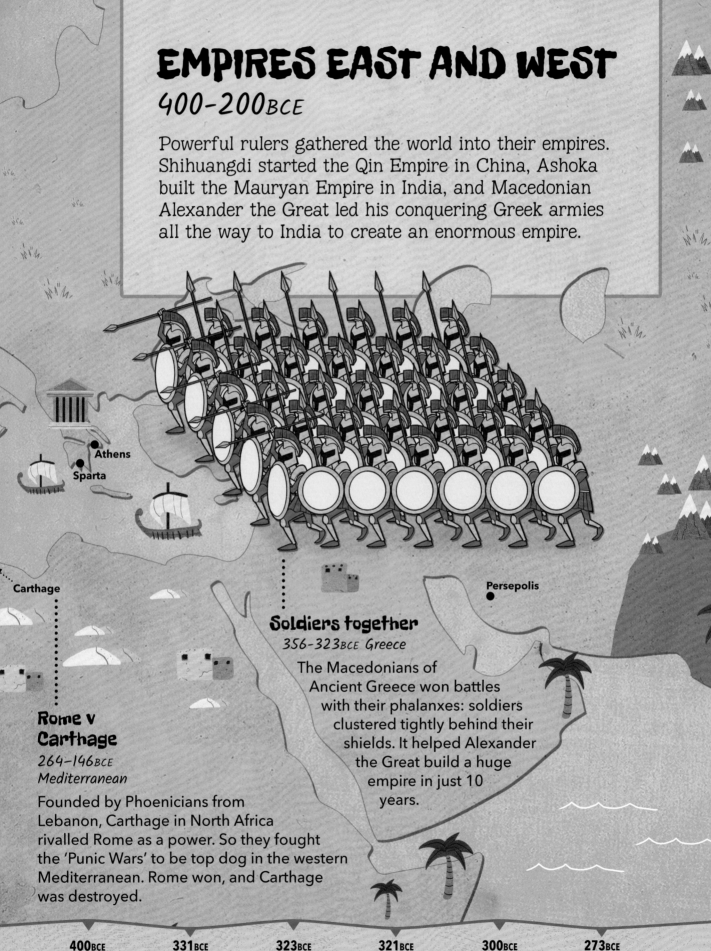

EMPIRES EAST AND WEST
400-200BCE

Powerful rulers gathered the world into their empires. Shihuangdi started the Qin Empire in China, Ashoka built the Mauryan Empire in India, and Macedonian Alexander the Great led his conquering Greek armies all the way to India to create an enormous empire.

Athens

Sparta

Carthage

Persepolis

Soldiers together
356-323BCE Greece

The Macedonians of Ancient Greece won battles with their phalanxes: soldiers clustered tightly behind their shields. It helped Alexander the Great build a huge empire in just 10 years.

Rome v Carthage
264-146BCE Mediterranean

Founded by Phoenicians from Lebanon, Carthage in North Africa rivalled Rome as a power. So they fought the 'Punic Wars' to be top dog in the western Mediterranean. Rome won, and Carthage was destroyed.

400BCE	**331BCE**	**323BCE**	**321BCE**	**300BCE**	**273BCE**
Celts continue moving to Britain from Germany	Alexander defeats the Persians	Death of Alexander the Great	Mauryan Empire begins in India	Largest pyramid built in Mexico	Ashoka becomes Mauryan emperor

Map key

- Alexander's Empire
- Mauryan Empire
- Qin Empire

Priest or warrior?

400BCE–1521CE Mexico

For 2,000 years, the Zapotec city of Monte Albán lorded it over southern Mexico. Their warrior-priests wore their victims' skins to battle.

Great Wall

220–206BCE China

How do you keep invaders out? Simple: build a wall. That's what the Chinese did. A Great Wall, nearly 9,000 km long! Shihuangdi built a famous version, but the wall today dates mostly from the Ming period (1368-1644).

Xi'an

Pataliputra

What Ashoka

273–232BCE India

Ashoka the Great extended the Mauryan Empire created by his grandfather Chandraguptar. He was a Buddhist and left instructions for living a good life carved on pillars throughout the empire.

Clay soldiers

210BCE China

Shihuangdi, the first Chinese emperor, unified the country. For his tomb he had a lifesize army built from terracotta (clay): 8,000 soldiers, 670 horses and 130 chariots.

264BCE	257BCE	221BCE	206BCE	200BCE	200BCE
Wars start between Rome and Carthage	Thuc Dynasty in Vietnam	Shihuangdi ends civil war in China	China-Europe Silk Road flourishes	Paper invented in China	Maya city of El Mirador flourishes

Hadrian's Wall
122CE Britain

In 53BCE, Julius Caesar launched the Roman conquest of Britain, which took over 90 years to achieve. But the Romans never conquered the tough Picts in Scotland. Emperor Hadrian built a wall across England to keep them out!

Londinium (London)

Herman's Germans
9CE Teutoborg

Germanic tribes led by Arminius (Herman) bashed the Roman army in a storm in the Teutoborg Forest. It was Rome's worst defeat and stopped them taking over Northern Europe.

GAUL

Lugdunum (Lyon)

Rome

Pompeii

Sun worship
200CE Mexico

For 600 years, Teotihuacán was the largest city in the Americas. It was dominated by a pyramid, which the Aztecs later called Pyramid of the Sun, but no one knows its original name.

Teotihuacán

Volcano disaster
79CE Italy

The Roman city of Pompeii was buried by scorching ash falling from the eruption of the volcano Vesuvius. Thousands were killed, but the ash preserved the city for 2,000 years.

200BCE	146BCE	c.100BCE	70BCE	58-50BCE	49BCE
Hopewell culture in North America	Carthage destroyed by Rome	Chola empire starts in India	Jerusalem temple destroyed by Rome	Caesar's Gallic Wars in France	Roman civil war begins

Mad emperors

37-41CE (Caligula), 54-68CE (Nero) Rome

Caligula and Nero were the maddest emperors - so their enemies said. Both liked wild parties. Caligula wanted his horse to be in the government. And Nero set Rome on fire…

You're so rugged!

48BCE Alexandria, Egypt

When Caesar arrived in Egypt, young Queen Cleopatra needed his help to win her throne back from her brother. So she had herself delivered to him rolled in a carpet. They soon became lovers.

Hans on

206BCE-220CE China

Under the Han emperors, Chinese life was sophisticated, with many clever inventions such as paper, the compass and a device for detecting earthquakes. People at court wore luxurious silk clothes.

Daxing

CHINA

Map key

Roman Empire

Alexandria

EGYPT

ROMAN MIGHT

200BCE–200CE

In 44BCE, the great Roman general Julius Caesar was assassinated. The Roman Republic ended, and Caesar's adopted son became Emperor Augustus. Soon Rome's tough and highly disciplined armies won a vast empire across Europe and the Mediterranean.

44BCE	27BCE	6-4BCE	3CE	9CE	79CE
Caesar assassinated	Roman Empire begins	Birth of Jesus Christ	Imperial University in Han China	Romans defeated at Teutoborg	Pompeii destroyed by Vesuvius

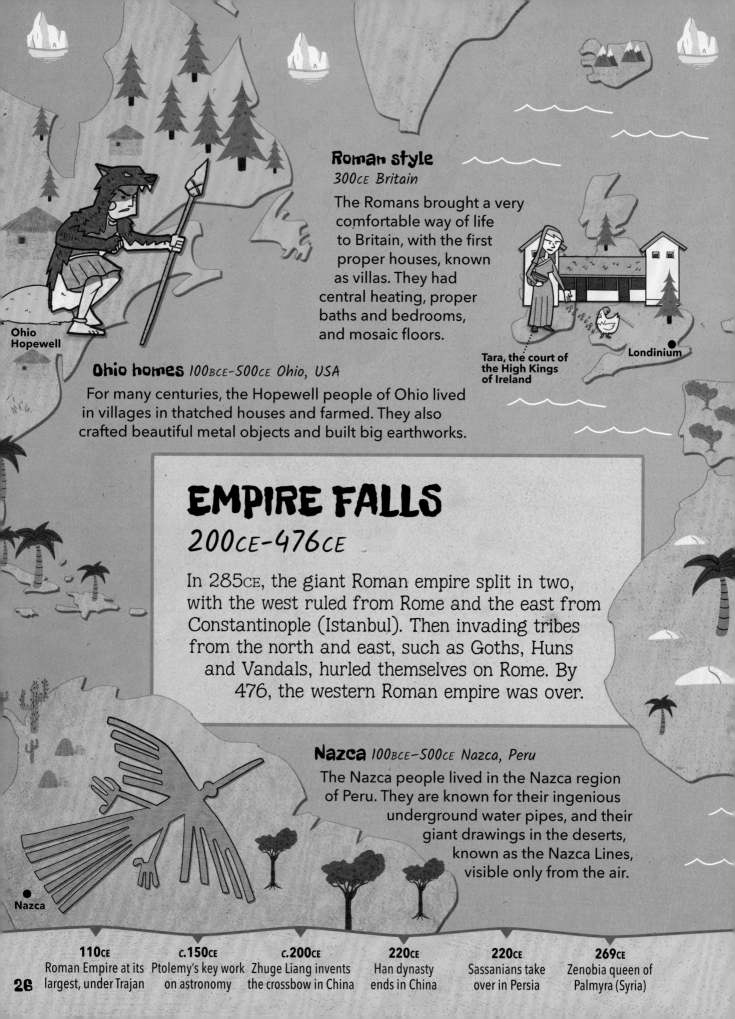

Roman style
300CE Britain

The Romans brought a very comfortable way of life to Britain, with the first proper houses, known as villas. They had central heating, proper baths and bedrooms, and mosaic floors.

Ohio Hopewell

Ohio homes *100BCE–500CE Ohio, USA*

For many centuries, the Hopewell people of Ohio lived in villages in thatched houses and farmed. They also crafted beautiful metal objects and built big earthworks.

Tara, the court of the High Kings of Ireland

Londinium

EMPIRE FALLS
200CE–476CE

In 285CE, the giant Roman empire split in two, with the west ruled from Rome and the east from Constantinople (Istanbul). Then invading tribes from the north and east, such as Goths, Huns and Vandals, hurled themselves on Rome. By 476, the western Roman empire was over.

Nazca *100BCE–500CE Nazca, Peru*

The Nazca people lived in the Nazca region of Peru. They are known for their ingenious underground water pipes, and their giant drawings in the deserts, known as the Nazca Lines, visible only from the air.

Nazca

110CE	**c.150CE**	**c.200CE**	**220CE**	**220CE**	**269CE**
Roman Empire at its largest, under Trajan	Ptolemy's key work on astronomy	Zhuge Liang invents the crossbow in China	Han dynasty ends in China	Sassanians take over in Persia	Zenobia queen of Palmyra (Syria)

Rome vandalized

410CE Rome

The fearsome Visigoths led by their king, Alaric, rode into Rome in 410CE and wrecked it. The Vandals did the same 45 years later. Then in 476CE, the Ostrogoths invaded and Rome was finished.

GAUL

Constantinople

Rome

ANATOLIA

SASSANID PERSIAN EMPIRE

Leptis magna, Libya

Three-way split

220-280CE China

After the Hans fell, China was split into three kingdoms: Shu, Wu and Wei. In a fictional story, three heroes – the Shu emperor, Liu Bei, and his generals Guan Yu and Zhang Fei, swore a famous oath to each other under a peach tree.

Crossroads *312CE Constantinople (Istanbul)*

Constantine was the first Christian emperor. Legend says he converted when he saw a cross before a crucial battle. He briefly unified the east and west empires but ruled from Constantinople, named after him.

Invasions

400-700CE Central Europe

For centuries, wave after wave of wild Germanic tribes invaded from the north in bands 10-20,000 strong, often on horses. They included Goths, Anglo-Saxons, Vandals and Franks. The Huns, led by Attila, came in from the east.

Anglo-Saxons
Franks
Goths
Visigoths
Ostrogoths
Huns
Vandals

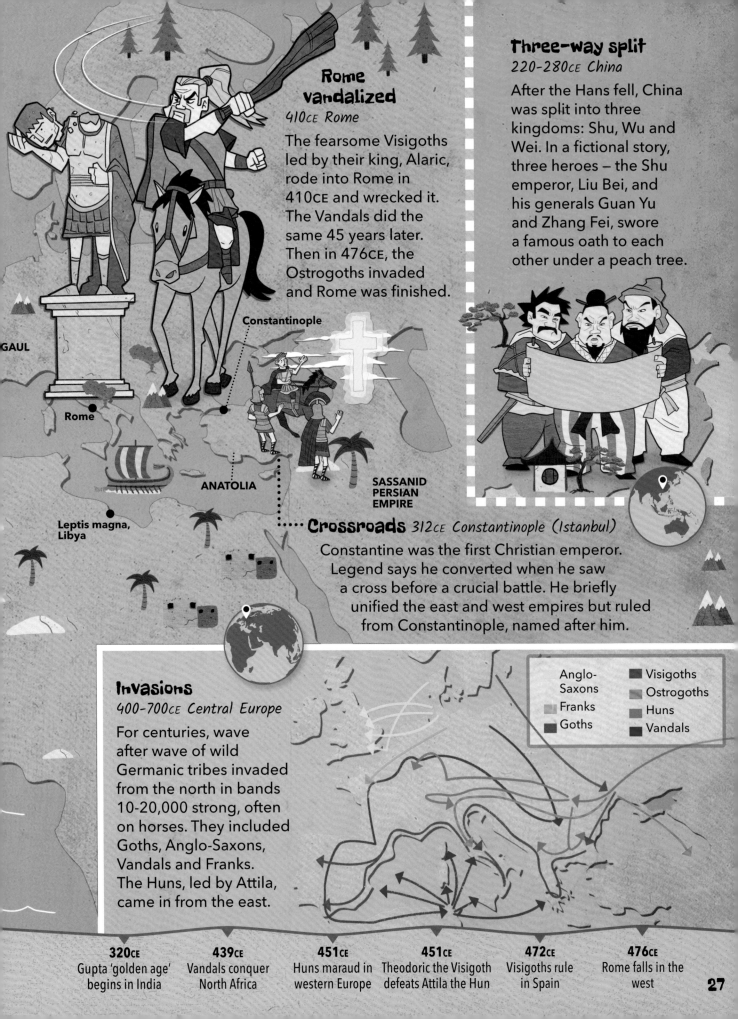

320CE	439CE	451CE	451CE	472CE	476CE
Gupta 'golden age' begins in India	Vandals conquer North Africa	Huns maraud in western Europe	Theodoric the Visigoth defeats Attila the Hun	Visigoths rule in Spain	Rome falls in the west

WHO'S WHO

Ancient history was full of all kinds of peoples. Some of them are superfamous like the Ancient Egyptians. Some of them are long forgotten in the mists of time. Here are a few you have encountered in this book.

You've got a point: Clovis
13,000 years ago

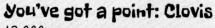

The Clovis of New Mexico were the first known people in North America, known by their stone spearheads or 'Clovis points'.

13,000 ya

Let's be civil: Sumerians
4500-2004BCE

The Sumerians lived in what is now southern Iraq and were the world's first great civilization. They invented writing and the wheel.

Carry on Carthage: Carthaginians
814-146BCE

Founded by the Phoenicians from Lebanon in what is now Tunisia, Carthage became a powerful trading city and a rival to the Greeks in Sicily, and to Rome.

Zap them: Zapotecs
700BCE-1400CE

The Zapotec civilization of Oaxaca, Mexico developed the first American writing.

Classic! Ancient Greeks
500BCE-323BCE

Centred on Athens, the Ancient Greeks changed the world with their brilliant ideas on philosophy and science, their drama and their elegant temples and statues.

Rome everywhere: Ancient Romans
753BCE-476CE

For 500 years, the city of Rome was a republic, but from 27BCE, its disciplined army carved out a huge empire, dominated by world-changing architecture and technology.

Horsey people: Scythians
900-100BCE

The Scythians lived in what is now Ukraine and Kazakhstan. They were nomadic people and were among the first to fight on horseback.

Purring Persians
550BCE-651CE

Cyrus the Great united the Persian people of what is now Iran to create an empire that became Rome's main rival. It was noted for its luxury and high-speed messenger service.

I want my mummy: Ancient Egyptians
3100–332BCE

The Ancient Egyptians built their great civilization on the River Nile and were ruled by Pharaohs. They are famous for their pyramids and mummies.

Artsy Akkadians
2334–2154BCE

The Akkadians ruled in Mesopotamia (in modern Iraq). They were related to the Sumerians and introduced the first postal service.

Awesome Assyrians
2450–612BCE

The Assyrian Empire was the most powerful and enduring of all the civilizations of the Middle East. The Assyrians were known as cruel, skilled soldiers and great builders.

Horsedrawn Hittites
1600–1180BCE

The Hittites were based in hilltop cities in Anatolia (Turkey) and built an empire with chariots and their skilful use of iron for weapons.

Mighty Maya
c.350BCE–1697CE

The Maya civilization of southern Central America lasted almost 4,000 years. The Maya built pyramids and invented the only complete American writing system.

Big shippers: Phoenicians
1500–300BCE

The Phoenicians came from city ports in Lebanon, such as Tyre and Sidon, and traded by sea far across the Mediterranean.

Head strong: Olmec
1600–400BCE

Famous for building huge stone heads, the Olmec of southern Mexico was the first great American civilization.

Metalsmiths: Celts
750–12BCE

The Celts were a warlike people who lived mainly in central and northwest Europe. They were very skilled at metalworking and making jewellery.

Gothic horror: Goths
394–775CE

The Goths were Germanic people who migrated west from their homelands around the Baltic to invade the Roman Empire. There were two main groups: Visigoths (western Goths) and Ostrogoths (eastern Goths).

775CE

WELL I NEVER...

Some strange stories from
ancient history

RAMESSES THE BIG

Egyptian pharaoh
Ramesses II was called
the Great because
he was, they said,
so awesome. But it
was mostly PR. He
presented his close-
shave battle against the
Hittites as a stunning
victory. And erected
huge statues of himself,
which are now often
buried in sand.

GOING FOR A PUNT

The Egyptian Queen
Hatshepsut told us all
about the amazing land
of Punt. If they wanted
incense, ebony or
gold, they rattled off an
expedition to Punt. But
no one knows if there
really was such a place.
The only evidence
is the oar from an
expedition boat on the
shores of the Red Sea.

I SAID PACK YOUR TRUNKS...

In 218BCE, Carthaginian general Hannibal
caught Rome by surprise by attacking from
the North. But that meant leading all his
army – including his trained elephants –
over the Alps. And there were no roads then,
just narrow, super-slippery paths and deadly
cliffs. Astonishingly, he did it!

KNOT ME

In 333BCE, Alexander the Great and his army reached the city of Gordium (in modern Turkey). A famous chariot was tied up by an intricate knot. They said: 'Only the conqueror of Asia can untie that knot!' Alexander didn't mess around. He just slashed the knot with his sword…

I AM SPARTACUS

Spartacus was a Roman slave forced to train as a gladiator: a warrior who had to fight to the death in the arena for entertainment. In 73BCE, he escaped and led an army of slaves into the hills. Soon their army was 100,000 strong. But eventually the rebellion was crushed, and Spartacus and many of the slaves were crucified.

JUST A WORM IN A TEACUP

According to Chinese legend, Empress Hsi Ling Shih was sipping tea under a mulberry tree, when a silkworm cocoon fell into her cup and unravelled in shimmering threads of silk. Silkworms are the larvae of silk moths. The empress found out how to cultivate the moths to make silk. Rich Chinese wore this luxurious fabric and it was long carried across Asia to the rich in Europe on the Silk Road.

INDEX

The Author

John Farndon is Royal Literary Fellow at City&Guilds in London, UK, and the author of a huge number of books for adults and children on science, technology and history, including international best-sellers. He has been shortlisted six times for the Royal Society's Young People's Book Prize, with titles such as *How the Earth Works* and *What Happens When?*

The Illustrator

Italian-born Christian Cornia decided at the age of four to be a comic-book artist, and is essentially self-taught. He works digitally, but always has a sketchbook in his bag. Christian has illustrated Marvel Comics and is one of the artists for the Scooby-Doo character in Italy and the USA. He also teaches animation at the Scuola Internazionale di Comics in Italy.